Woodland Creatures
Backpacks

Create fun carryalls for kids with these
five cute appliquéd animals! Some include
dimensional accents such as tails, legs, wings, or ears.

LEISURE ARTS, INC. • Maumelle, Arkansas

Filomena Fox

Our instructions include binding the raw edges of the seam allowances inside your backpack for a tidy finished look. To make your project faster and easier, you may zigzag or serge these edges.

Finished Size: 9½" x 12½" x 5" (24 cm x 32 cm x 13 cm)

SHOPPING LIST

Yardage is based on 43"/44" (109 cm/112 cm) wide fabric with a usable width of 40" (102 cm).

☐ 1 yd (91 cm) of turquoise print fabric for backpack body, backpack bottom, zipper opening, straps, and handle loop

☐ ³/₈ yd (34 cm) of gold print fabric for head, ears, body, and tail

☐ ¼ yd (23 cm) of white solid fabric for inner ears, face, and chest

☐ scrap of black solid fabric for eyes and nose

☐ 1¼ yds (1.1 m) of fabric for lining

☐ 2⁵/₈ yds (2.4 m) of 20" (51 cm) wide woven fusible interfacing (such as Pellon® SF 101)

☐ ⁵/₈ yd (57 cm) of 45" (114 cm) wide fusible fleece (such as Pellon® 987F)

☐ ³/₄ yd (69 cm) of 15" (38 cm) wide paper-backed fusible web (such as Pellon® Wonder Under® 805)

☐ 20" (51 cm) turquoise zipper

☐ two 1" (25 mm) white side-release buckles

☐ black thread for appliqué

☐ Glad® Press and Seal® Wrap

☐ Sharpie® fine-point permanent marker

☐ disappearing ink fabric marker

☐ stabilizer

CUTTING THE PIECES

*Follow **Rotary Cutting**, page 30, to cut fabric. All measurements include seam allowances. Patterns are on pages 16-17 and 20-22.*

From turquoise print fabric:
- Cut 2 **backpack bodies** 11" x 14".
- Cut 2 **lower straps** 4" x 12½".
- Cut 2 **upper straps** 4" x 10½".
- Cut 2 **zipper flaps** 3" x 20½".
- Cut **bottom** 5½" x 19½".
- Cut **handle loop** 4" x 8".
- Cut 2 **zipper ends** 2" x 8".

From gold print fabric:
- Use pattern, page 21, to cut 1 **tail (J)** and 1 **tail (J)** in reverse.

From lining fabric:
- Cut 2 *bias* binding strips 2½" x 45".
- Cut 2 **backpack body linings** 11" x 14".
- Cut **bottom lining** 5½" x 19½".
- Cut 2 **zipper flap linings** 3" x 20½".
- Cut 2 **pockets** 7½" x 12".

From fusible interfacing:
- Cut 4 **backpack bodies** 11" x 14".
- Cut 4 **zipper flaps** 3" x 20½".
- Cut 2 **bottoms** 5½" x 19".
- Cut 2 **lower straps** 4" x 12".
- Cut 2 **upper straps** 4" x 10".
- Cut **handle loop** 4" x 8".

From fusible fleece:
- Cut 2 **backpack bodies** 11" x 14".
- Cut **bottom** 5½" x 19".

CUTTING THE APPLIQUÉS

*Follow **Preparing Fusible Appliqués**, page 31, to use patterns.* **Note:** *Appliqué patterns are printed in reverse.*

From gold print fabric:
- Cut **body (A)**.
- Cut 1 **ear (C)**; cut 1 **ear (C)** in reverse.
- Cut **head (E)**.

From white solid fabric:
- Cut **chest (B)**.
- Cut 1 **inner ear (D)**; cut 1 **inner ear (D)** in reverse.
- Cut **face (F)**.
- Cut 1 **tail tip (I)**; cut 1 **tail tip (I)** in reverse.

From black solid fabric:
- Cut 2 **eyes (G)**.
- Cut **nose (H)**.

MAKING THE TAIL

*Follow **Satin Stitch Appliqué**, page 31, for appliqué instructions. Follow **Machine Sewing** and **Pressing**, page 31, to make the backpack. Match right sides and use ¼" seam allowances unless otherwise indicated.*

1. Referring to the **Diagram**, page 20, arrange one tail tip (I) appliqué on one tail (J); fuse in place.
2. Satin Stitch appliqué the tail tip to the tail along the upper edge.
3. Repeat Steps 1-2 for the remaining tail.
4. Leaving straight top edge open for turning, sew 2 tails together.
5. Clip curves and corners and turn tail right side out; press.
6. Set tail aside.

PREPARING THE BACKPACK BODY AND LINING PIECES

1. Place the fusible interfacing **backpack body**, fusible side down, on the wrong side of one turquoise print **backpack body**; fuse.
2. Repeat Step 1 to prepare the remaining turquoise print backpack body and two **backpack body linings**.
3. Place the fusible fleece **backpack body**, fusible side down, on the wrong side of one interfaced backpack body; fuse to prepare the backpack body front.

4. Repeat Step 3 to prepare the backpack body back.
5. Use the backpack body pattern, pages 16-17, to cut the backpack body from the fleece-lined backpack body front and back and two backpack body linings.
6. Refer to Fig. 1 to baste the tail to the lower edge of the backpack body back.

Fig. 1

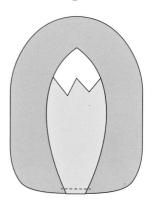

ADDING THE APPLIQUÉS

1. Referring to the **Diagram**, page 20, arrange the appliqués on the backpack body front; fuse in place.
2. Satin Stitch appliqués to backpack body front.
3. Using the face (F) pattern, trace the mouth details on non-sticky side of plastic wrap. Layer the plastic wrap on the appliquéd face; Satin Stitch along drawn lines. Remove the plastic wrap.

COMPLETING THE BACKPACK

1. Refer to **Assembling the Backpack**, page 12, to complete the backpack.

Fitzgerald Frog

Our instructions include binding the raw edges of the seam allowances inside your backpack for a tidy finished look. To make your project faster and easier, you may zigzag or serge these edges.

Finished Size: 9¹/₂" x 12¹/₂" x 5" (24 cm x 32 cm x 13 cm)

SHOPPING LIST

Yardage is based on 43"/44" (109 cm/112 cm) wide fabric with a usable width of 40" (102 cm).

☐ ⁷/₈ yd (80 cm) of turquoise print fabric for backpack body, zipper opening, straps, and handle loop

☐ ³/₈ yd (34 cm) of green small print fabric for backpack bottom, frog body, and head

☐ ¹/₄ yd (23 cm) of green medium print fabric for frog legs

☐ scrap of white solid fabric for eyes

☐ 1¹/₄ yds (1.1 m) of fabric for lining

☐ 2⁵/₈ yds (2.4 m) of 20" (51 cm) wide woven fusible interfacing (such as Pellon® SF 101)

☐ ⁵/₈ yd (57 cm) of 45" (114 cm) wide fusible fleece (such as Pellon® 987F)

☐ ¹/₂ yd (46 cm) of 15" (38 cm) wide paper-backed fusible web (such as Pellon® Wonder Under® 805)

☐ 20" (51 cm) turquoise zipper

☐ two 1" (25 mm) turquoise side-release buckles

☐ black thread for appliqué

☐ Glad® Press and Seal® Wrap

☐ Sharpie® fine-point permanent marker

☐ two ⁷/₁₆" (11 mm) diameter black buttons

☐ disappearing ink fabric marker

☐ stabilizer

CUTTING THE PIECES

*Follow **Rotary Cutting**, page 30, to cut fabric. All measurements include seam allowances. Patterns are on pages 16-17 and 26-28.*

From turquoise print fabric:
- Cut 2 **backpack bodies** 11" x 14".
- Cut 2 **lower straps** 4" x 12½".
- Cut 2 **upper straps** 4" x 10½".
- Cut 2 **zipper flaps** 3" x 20½".
- Cut **handle loop** 4" x 8".
- Cut 2 **zipper ends** 2" x 8".

From green small print fabric:
- Cut **bottom** 5½" x 19½".

From green medium print fabric:
- Use pattern, page 28, to cut 2 **frog legs (E)** and 2 **frog legs (E)** in reverse.

From lining fabric:
- Cut 2 *bias* binding strips 2½" x 45".
- Cut 2 **backpack body linings** 11" x 14".
- Cut **bottom lining** 5½" x 19½".
- Cut 2 **zipper flap linings** 3" x 20½".
- Cut 2 **pockets** 7½" x 12".

From fusible interfacing:
- Cut 4 **backpack bodies** 11" x 14".
- Cut 4 **zipper flaps** 3" x 20½".
- Cut 2 **bottoms** 5½" x 19".
- Cut 2 **lower straps** 4" x 12".
- Cut 2 **upper straps** 4" x 10".
- Cut **handle loop** 4" x 8".

From fusible fleece:
- Cut 2 **backpack bodies** 11" x 14".
- Cut **bottom** 5½" x 19".

CUTTING THE APPLIQUÉS

*Follow **Preparing Fusible Appliqués**, page 31, to use patterns.* **Note:** *Appliqué patterns are printed in reverse.*

From green small print fabric:
- Cut **frog body (A)**.
- Cut **head (B)**.

From green medium print fabric:
- Cut 1 **frog leg (C)** and 1 **frog leg (C)** in reverse.

From white solid fabric:
- Cut **eyes (D)**.

MAKING THE LEGS

*Follow **Machine Sewing** and **Pressing**, page 31, to make the backpack. Match right sides and use ¼" seam allowances unless otherwise indicated.*

1. Leaving straight top edge open for turning, sew 2 **frog legs (E)** together.
2. Clip curves and corners and turn leg right side out; press.
3. Repeat Steps 1-2 for remaining leg.
4. Set legs aside.

PREPARING THE BACKPACK BODY AND LINING PIECES

1. Place the fusible interfacing **backpack body**, fusible side down, on the wrong side of one turquoise print **backpack body**; fuse.
2. Repeat Step 1 to prepare the remaining turquoise print backpack body and two **backpack body linings**.
3. Place the fusible fleece **backpack body**, fusible side down, on the wrong side of one interfaced backpack body; fuse to prepare the backpack body front.

4. Repeat Step 3 to prepare the backpack body back.
5. Use the backpack body pattern, pages 16-17, to cut the backpack body from the fleece-lined backpack body front and back and two backpack body linings.
6. Refer to **Fig. 1** to baste the frog legs to the lower edge of the backpack body back.

Fig. 1

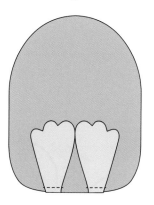

ADDING THE APPLIQUÉS

*Follow **Satin Stitch Appliqué**, page 31, for appliqué instructions.*

1. Referring to the **Diagram**, page 26, arrange the appliqués on the backpack body front; fuse in place.
2. Satin Stitch appliqués to backpack body front.
3. Using the head (**B**) pattern, trace the eyebrows and mouth details on non-sticky side of plastic wrap. Layer the plastic wrap on the appliquéd face; Satin Stitch along drawn lines. Remove the plastic wrap.
4. Sew the buttons to the eyes.

COMPLETING THE BACKPACK

1. Refer to **Assembling the Backpack**, page 12, to complete the backpack.

Bryson Bear

Our instructions include binding the raw edges of the seam allowances inside your backpack for a tidy finished look. To make your project faster and easier, you may zigzag or serge these edges.

Finished Size: 9¹/₂" x 12¹/₂" x 5" (24 cm x 32 cm x 13 cm)

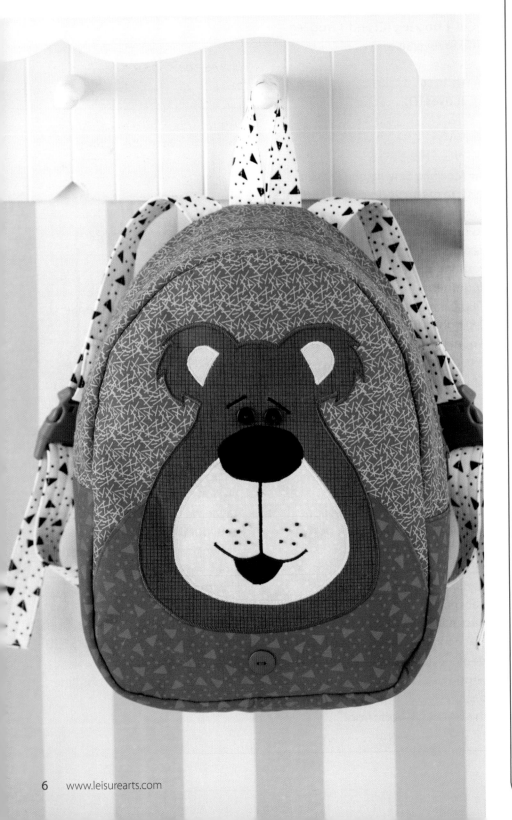

Yardage is based on 43"/44" (109 cm/112 cm) wide fabric with a usable width of 40" (102 cm).

- ☐ ⁵/₈ yd (57 cm) of blue print fabric for backpack body and zipper opening
- ☐ ¹/₄ yd (23 cm) of black and white print fabric for handle loop and straps
- ☐ ¹/₄ yd (23 cm) of red print fabric for backpack bottom and bear shirt
- ☐ 8" x 10¹/₂" (20 cm x 27 cm) scrap of brown print fabric for head
- ☐ 6" x 6" (15 cm x 15 cm) piece of tan print fabric for snout
- ☐ scraps of black solid fabric for nose and mouth and pink solid fabric for ears
- ☐ 1¹/₄ yds (1.1 m) of fabric for lining
- ☐ 2⁵/₈ yds (2.4 m) of 20" (51 cm) wide woven fusible interfacing (such as Pellon® SF 101)
- ☐ ⁵/₈ yd (57 cm) of 45" (114 cm) wide fusible fleece (such as Pellon® 987F)
- ☐ ³/₄ yd (69 cm) of 15" (38 cm) wide paper-backed fusible web (such as Pellon® Wonder Under® 805)
- ☐ 20" (51 cm) blue zipper
- ☐ two 1" (25 mm) red side-release buckles
- ☐ black and coordinating threads for appliqué
- ☐ Glad® Press and Seal® Wrap
- ☐ Sharpie® fine-point permanent marker
- ☐ black embroidery floss
- ☐ embroidery needle
- ☐ two ⁷/₁₆" (11 mm) diameter black buttons and one ³/₄" (19 mm) diameter blue button
- ☐ disappearing ink fabric marker
- ☐ stabilizer

CUTTING THE PIECES

*Follow **Rotary Cutting**, page 30, to cut fabric. All measurements include seam allowances. Patterns are on pages 16-19.*

From blue print fabric:
- Cut 2 **backpack bodies** 11" x 14".
- Cut 2 **zipper flaps** 3" x 20½".
- Cut 2 **zipper ends** 2" x 8".

From black and white print fabric:
- Cut 2 **lower straps** 4" x 12½".
- Cut 2 **upper straps** 4" x 10½".
- Cut **handle loop** 4" x 8".

From red print fabric:
- Cut **bottom** 5½" x 19½".

From lining fabric:
- Cut 2 *bias* binding strips 2½" x 45".
- Cut 2 **backpack body linings** 11" x 14".
- Cut **bottom lining** 5½" x 19½".
- Cut 2 **zipper flap linings** 3" x 20½".
- Cut 2 **pockets** 7½" x 12".

From fusible interfacing:
- Cut 4 **backpack bodies** 11" x 14".
- Cut 4 **zipper flaps** 3" x 20½".
- Cut 2 **bottoms** 5½" x 19".
- Cut 2 **lower straps** 4" x 12".
- Cut 2 **upper straps** 4" x 10".
- Cut **handle loop** 4" x 8".

From fusible fleece:
- Cut 2 **backpack bodies** 11" x 14".
- Cut **bottom** 5½" x 19".

CUTTING THE APPLIQUÉS

*Follow **Preparing Fusible Appliqués**, page 31, to use patterns. **Note:** Appliqué patterns are printed in reverse.*

From red print fabric:
- Cut 1 **shirt (A)**.

From brown print fabric:
- Cut 1 **head (B)**.

From tan print fabric:
- Cut 1 **snout (C)**.

From black solid fabric:
- Cut 1 **nose (D)**.
- Cut 1 **mouth (E)**.

From pink solid fabric:
- Cut 1 **ear (F)**; cut 1 **ear (F)** in reverse.

PREPARING THE BACKPACK BODY AND LINING PIECES

1. Place the fusible interfacing **backpack body**, fusible side down, on the wrong side of one blue print **backpack body**; fuse.
2. Repeat Step 1 to prepare the remaining blue print backpack body and two **backpack body linings**.
3. Place a fusible fleece **backpack body**, fusible side down, on the wrong side of one interfaced backpack body; fuse to prepare the backpack body front.
4. Repeat Step 3 to prepare the remaining backpack body back.
5. Use the backpack body pattern, pages 16-17, to cut the backpack body from the fleece-lined backpack body front and back and two backpack body linings.

ADDING THE APPLIQUÉS

*Follow **Satin Stitch Appliqué**, page 31, for appliqué instructions.*

1. Referring to the **Diagram**, page 18, arrange the appliqués on the backpack body front; fuse in place.
2. Satin Stitch appliqués to backpack body front.

3. Using the head (**B**) and snout (**C**) patterns, trace the eyebrow and snout details on non-sticky side of plastic wrap. Layer the plastic wrap on the appliquéd face; Satin Stitch along drawn lines. Remove the plastic wrap.
4. Using six strands of floss, add French Knots to snout.

COMPLETING THE BACKPACK

*Follow **Machine Sewing** and **Pressing**, page 31, to make the backpack. Match right sides and use a ¼" seam allowance unless otherwise indicated.*

1. Refer to **Assembling the Backpack**, page 12, to complete the backpack.
2. Sew the buttons to the bear for eyes.
3. Sew the button to the shirt.

FRENCH KNOT

Bring needle up at 1. Wrap thread around needle. Insert needle at 2, tighten knot, and pull needle through fabric, holding thread until it must be released (*Fig. 1*).

Fig. 1

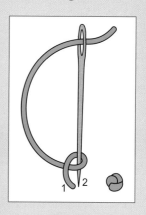

Thomas Turtle

Our instructions include binding the raw edges of the
seam allowances inside your backpack for a tidy finished look.
To make your project faster and easier, you may zigzag or serge these edges.

Finished Size: 9¹/₂" x 12¹/₂" x 5" (24 cm x 32 cm x 13 cm)

SHOPPING LIST

Yardage is based on 43"/44" (109 cm/112 cm) wide fabric with a usable width of 40" (102 cm).

- ☐ ⁵/₈ yd (57 cm) of green large print fabric for backpack body and zipper opening
- ☐ ¹/₄ yd (23 cm) of turquoise print fabric for backpack body trim and bottom
- ☐ ¹/₄ yd (23 cm) of teal print fabric for appliqués
- ☐ ³/₈ yd (34 cm) of purple print fabric for appliqués, straps, and handle loop
- ☐ ¹/₄ yd (23 cm) of green small print fabric for appliqués
- ☐ scrap of white solid fabric for eyes
- ☐ 1¹/₄ yds (1.1 m) of fabric for lining
- ☐ 2⁵/₈ yds (2.4 m) of 20" (51 cm) wide woven fusible interfacing (such as Pellon® SF 101)
- ☐ ⁵/₈ yd (57 cm) of 45" (114 cm) wide fusible fleece (such as Pellon® 987F)
- ☐ ³/₄ yd (69 cm) of 15" (38 cm) wide paper-backed fusible web (such as Pellon® Wonder Under® 805)
- ☐ 20" (51 cm) green zipper
- ☐ two 1" (25 mm) green side-release buckles
- ☐ black and coordinating thread for appliqué
- ☐ Glad® Press and Seal® Wrap
- ☐ Sharpie® fine-point permanent marker
- ☐ two ¹/₄" (6 mm) diameter black ball buttons
- ☐ disappearing ink fabric marker
- ☐ stabilizer

CUTTING THE PIECES

*Follow **Rotary Cutting**, page 30, to cut fabric. All measurements include seam allowances. Patterns are on pages 16-17 and 23-25.*

From green large print fabric:
- Cut 2 **backpack bodies** 11" x 14".
- Cut 2 **zipper flaps** 3" x 20 1/2".
- Cut 2 **zipper ends** 2" x 8".

From turquoise print fabric:
- Cut **bottom** 5 1/2" x 19 1/2".
- Cut **backpack body trim** 11" x 3".

From purple print fabric:
- Cut 2 **upper straps** 4" x 10 1/2".
- Cut 2 **lower straps** 4" x 12 1/2".
- Cut **handle loop** 4" x 8".

From lining fabric:
- Cut 2 *bias* binding strips 2 1/2" x 45".
- Cut 2 **backpack body linings** 11" x 14".
- Cut **bottom lining** 5 1/2" x 19 1/2".
- Cut 2 **zipper flap linings** 3" x 20 1/2".
- Cut 2 **pockets** 7 1/2" x 12".

From fusible interfacing:
- Cut 4 **backpack bodies** 11" x 14".
- Cut 4 **zipper flaps** 3" x 20 1/2".
- Cut 2 **bottoms** 5 1/2" x 19".
- Cut 2 **lower straps** 4" x 12".
- Cut 2 **upper straps** 4" x 10".
- Cut **handle loop** 4" x 8".

From fusible fleece:
- Cut 2 **backpack bodies** 11" x 14".
- Cut **bottom** 5 1/2" x 19".

CUTTING THE APPLIQUÉS

*Follow **Preparing Fusible Appliqués**, page 31, to use patterns.* **Note:** *Appliqué patterns are printed in reverse.*

From teal print fabric:
- Cut **shell (A)**.
- Cut **shell (B)**.
- Cut **shell (C)**.
- Cut **shell (D)**.
- Cut **shell (E)**.

From purple print fabric:
- Cut **shell (G)**.
- Cut **shell (H)**.
- Cut **shell (I)**.
- Cut **shell (J)**.
- Cut **shell (K)**.
- Cut **shell (L)**.
- Cut **shell (M)**.

From green small print fabric:
- Cut 1 **foot (F)**; cut 1 **foot (F)** in reverse.
- Cut **neck (N)**.
- Cut **head (O)**.

From white solid fabric:
- Cut 2 **eyes (P)**.

PREPARING THE BACKPACK BODY AND LINING PIECES

*Follow **Machine Sewing** and **Pressing**, page 31, to make the backpack. Match right sides and use 1/4" seam allowances unless otherwise indicated.*

1. Sew the **backpack body trim** to one short end of one **backpack body**. This is now the bottom edge.
2. Aligning bottom edges, place the fusible interfacing **backpack body**, fusible side down, on the wrong side of the pieced rectangle from Step 1; fuse.
3. Fuse interfacing backpack body to the wrong side of the remaining green print backpack body and two **backpack body linings**.

4. Aligning bottom edges, place a fusible fleece **backpack body**, fusible side down, on the wrong side of one interfaced backpack body; fuse to prepare the backpack body front.
5. Repeat Step 4 to prepare the backpack body back.
6. Aligning the line on the pattern with the seam on the backpack body front, use the backpack body pattern, pages 16-17, to cut the backpack body front from one fleece-lined backpack body. Use the pattern to cut the backpack body back from the remaining fleece-lined backpack body. Use the pattern to cut two backpack body linings.

ADDING THE APPLIQUÉS

*Follow **Satin Stitch Appliqué**, page 31, for appliqué instructions.*

1. Referring to the **Diagram**, page 23, arrange the appliqués on the backpack body front; fuse in place.
2. Satin Stitch appliqués to backpack body front.
3. Using the head pattern (**O**), trace the mouth detail on non-sticky side of plastic wrap. Layer the plastic wrap on the appliquéd face and freehand draw the eyebrows and glasses temples. Satin Stitch along drawn lines. Remove the plastic wrap.

COMPLETING THE BACKPACK

1. Refer to **Assembling the Backpack**, page 12, to complete the backpack.
2. Sew the buttons to the turtle for eyes.

9

Olympia Owl

Our instructions include binding the raw edges of the seam allowances inside your backpack for a tidy finished look. To make your project faster and easier, you may zigzag or serge these edges.

Finished Size: 9¹/₂" x 12¹/₂" x 5" (24 cm x 32 cm x 13 cm)

SHOPPING LIST

Yardage is based on 43"/44" (109 cm/112 cm) wide fabric with a usable width of 40" (102 cm).

- ☐ ¹/₂ yd (46 cm) of orange print fabric for backpack body
- ☐ ³/₈ yd (34 cm) of pink print fabric for backpack bottom and owl chest
- ☐ ¹/₄ yd (23 cm) of green print fabric for zipper opening
- ☐ ¹/₂ yd (46 cm) of turquoise print fabric for straps, handle loop, outer ears, eyes, and wings
- ☐ ¹/₄ yd (23 cm) of yellow print fabric for inner ears, beak, and feet
- ☐ scraps of white solid and black solid fabrics for eyes
- ☐ 1¹/₄ yds (1.1 m) of fabric for lining
- ☐ 2⁵/₈ yds (2.4 m) of 20" (51 cm) wide woven fusible interfacing (such as Pellon® SF 101)
- ☐ ⁵/₈ yd (57 cm) of 45" (114 cm) wide fusible fleece (such as Pellon® 987F)
- ☐ ³/₈ yd (34 cm) of 15" (38 cm) wide paper-backed fusible web (such as Pellon® Wonder Under® 805)
- ☐ 20" (51 cm) green zipper
- ☐ two 1" (25 mm) white side-release buckles
- ☐ coordinating thread for appliqué
- ☐ two 1¹/₈" (29 mm) diameter purple buttons
- ☐ disappearing ink fabric marker
- ☐ stabilizer

CUTTING THE PIECES

Follow Rotary Cutting, page 30, to cut fabric. Cut all strips from the selvage-to-selvage width of the fabric. All measurements include seam allowances. Patterns are on pages 16-17 and 28-29.

From orange print fabric:
- Cut 2 **backpack bodies** 11" x 14".

From pink print fabric:
- Cut **bottom** 5$\frac{1}{2}$" x 19$\frac{1}{2}$".

From green print fabric:
- Cut 2 **zipper flaps** 3" x 20$\frac{1}{2}$".
- Cut 2 **zipper ends** 2" x 8".

From turquoise print fabric:
- Cut 2 **upper straps** 4" x 10$\frac{1}{2}$".
- Cut 2 **lower straps** 4" x 12$\frac{1}{2}$".
- Cut **handle loop** 4" x 8".
- Use pattern, page 28, to cut 2 **wings (H)** and 2 **wings (H)** in reverse.
- Use pattern, page 29, to cut 2 **ears (G)** and 2 **ears (G)** in reverse.

From yellow print fabric:
- Use pattern, page 29, to cut 2 **feet (I)** and 2 **feet (I)** in reverse.

From lining fabric:
- Cut 2 *bias* binding strips 2$\frac{1}{2}$" x 45".
- Cut 2 **backpack body linings** 11" x 14".
- Cut **bottom lining** 5$\frac{1}{2}$" x 19$\frac{1}{2}$".
- Cut 2 **zipper flap linings** 3" x 20$\frac{1}{2}$".
- Cut 2 **pockets** 7$\frac{1}{2}$" x 12".

From fusible interfacing:
- Cut 4 **backpack bodies** 11" x 14".
- Cut 4 **zipper flaps** 3" x 20$\frac{1}{2}$".
- Cut 2 **bottoms** 5$\frac{1}{2}$" x 19".
- Cut 2 **upper straps** 4" x 10".
- Cut 2 **lower straps** 4" x 12".
- Cut **handle loop** 4" x 8".

From fusible fleece:
- Cut 2 **backpack bodies** 11" x 14".
- Cut **bottom** 5$\frac{1}{2}$" x 19".

CUTTING THE APPLIQUÉS

Follow Preparing Fusible Appliqués, page 31, to use patterns. **Note:** *Appliqué patterns are printed in reverse.*

From pink print fabric:
- Cut **chest (D)**.

From turquoise print fabric:
- Cut 2 **eyes (A)**.

From yellow print fabric:
- Cut **beak (E)**.
- Cut 1 **inner ear (F)** and 1 **inner ear (F)** in reverse.

From white solid fabric:
- Cut 2 **eyes (B)**.

From black solid fabric:
- Cut 2 **eyes (C)**.

MAKING THE EARS, FEET, AND WINGS

Follow Machine Sewing and Pressing, page 31, to make the backpack. Match right sides and use $\frac{1}{4}$" seam allowances unless otherwise indicated. Follow Satin Stitch Appliqué, page 31, for appliqué instructions.

1. Referring to the **Diagram**, page 29, arrange one inner ear appliqué **(F)** on one ear **(G)**; fuse in place. Repeat with one inner ear **(F)** in reverse and one ear **(G)** in reverse.
2. Satin Stitch appliqué inner ear appliqués to ears.
3. Leaving curved edge open for turning, sew 1 ear **(G)** and 1 appliquéd ear together.
4. Clip curves and corners and turn ear right side out; press.

5. Repeat Steps 3-4 for remaining ear.
6. Leaving straight edge open for turning, sew 1 foot **(I)** and 1 foot **(I)** in reverse together.
7. Clip curves and corners and turn foot right side out; press.
8. Repeat Steps 6-7 for remaining foot.
9. Leaving an opening for turning, sew 1 wing **(H)** and 1 wing **(H)** in reverse together.
10. Clip curves and corners and turn wing right side out; press.
11. Repeat Steps 9-10 for remaining wing.
12. Set all pieces aside.

PREPARING THE BACKPACK BODY AND LINING PIECES

1. Place the fusible interfacing **backpack body**, fusible side down, on the wrong side of one orange print **backpack body**; fuse.
2. Repeat Step 1 to prepare the remaining orange print backpack body and two **backpack body linings**.
3. Place the fusible fleece **backpack body**, fusible side down, on the wrong side of one interfaced backpack body; fuse to prepare the backpack body front.
4. Repeat Step 3 to prepare the backpack body back.
5. Use the backpack body pattern, pages 16-17, to cut the backpack body from the fleece-lined backpack body front and back and two backpack body linings.

ADDING THE APPLIQUÉS

1. Referring to the **Diagram**, page 29, arrange the appliqués on the backpack body front; fuse in place.
2. Satin Stitch appliqués to backpack body front.
3. Refer to **Fig. 1** to baste the ears to the upper edge and the feet to the lower edge of the backpack body front.

Fig. 1

COMPLETING THE BACKPACK

1. Refer to **Assembling the Backpack** to complete the backpack.
2. Sewing through one button and one wing, attach wing to each side of backpack.

Assembling
the Backpack

Before assembling, refer to the project instructions to prepare the backpack body and lining pieces and to add the appliqués.

MAKING THE ZIPPER OPENING

*Follow **Machine Sewing** and **Pressing**, page 31, to make the backpack. Match right sides and use 1/4" seam allowances unless otherwise indicated.*

1. Place the fusible interfacing **zipper flap**, fusible side down, on the wrong side of one **zipper flap**; fuse.
2. Repeat Step 1 to prepare the remaining zipper flap and two **zipper flap linings**.
3. Trimming from each end, trim the zipper to 18 1/2" long, taking care not to cut off the zipper slide.
4. Matching wrong sides and short ends, press one **zipper end** in half. Open and press the short ends to the middle crease *(Fig. 1)*. Refold at the center crease *(Fig. 2)*. The zipper end should measure 2" x 2". Repeat to make another zipper end.

Fig. 1

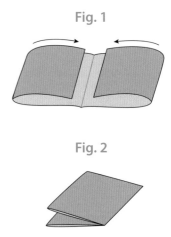

Fig. 2

5. Slip one zipper end onto one end of the zipper, overlapping the ends of the zipper by 1/2" *(Fig. 3)*. When sewing, pull zipper slide back slightly as needed to move slide out of the way. Sew through all layers close to the folded edges. Repeat for remaining end of zipper.

Fig. 3

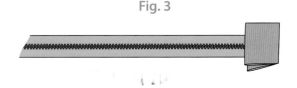

6. Trim sides of zipper ends even with width of the zipper tape. Centering zipper and trimming from each end, trim the zipper/ends to 20½" *(Fig. 4)*.

Fig. 4

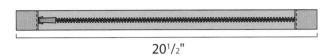

20½"

7. Place zipper/ends right side down on right side of one zipper flap. Using a zipper foot, sew zipper in place close to zipper teeth, zipping and unzipping as needed to move slide out of the way *(Fig. 5)*.

Fig. 5

8. Place remaining zipper flap lining, right side down on wrong side of zipper/ends with zipper/ends sandwiched in between. Sew the zipper flap lining to the zipper/ends *(Fig. 6)*.

Fig. 6

9. Press zipper flap and zipper flap lining away from zipper. Topstitch close to zipper *(Fig. 7)*.

Fig. 7

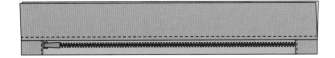

10. Repeat Steps 7-9 to sew remaining zipper flap and zipper flap lining to zipper.
11. Centering zipper, trim the zipper and flaps to 5½" x 19½". Baste a scant ¼" around all 4 sides, sewing zipper flap and zipper flap lining together *(Fig. 8)* to make zipper opening.

Fig. 8

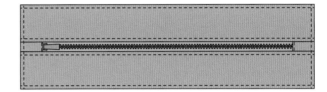

MAKING THE SIDES

1. Center the fusible interfacing **bottom**, fusible side down, on the wrong side of one **bottom**; fuse. The interfacing is ¼" shorter on each end.
2. Repeat Step 1 with the **bottom lining**.
3. Center and fuse the fusible fleece **bottom**, fusible side down, on the wrong side of the interfaced bottom. The fleece is ¼" shorter on each end.
4. Matching short ends, place zipper opening right side down on right side of bottom. Place the bottom lining right side down on the wrong side of the zipper opening. The zipper opening is sandwiched between the bottom and bottom lining. The wrong sides of the outer fabrics should be facing out. Sew across the short ends, making a loop. Press seam allowances away from zipper. Turn so that lining side is facing outward *(Fig. 9)*.

Fig. 9

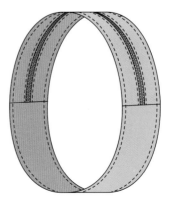

5. Baste along raw edges with a scant ¼" seam allowance. This is now the backpack sides.

6. Topstitch close to each seam on bottom. Matching the seams, fold the side in half and mark center top and bottom with a pin or disappearing ink fabric marker; set aside.

MAKING THE STRAPS AND HANDLE LOOP

1. Place the fusible interfacing **upper strap**, fusible side down, on the wrong side of one **upper strap**, leaving ½" on one end of strap; fuse.

2. Press non-interfaced end of upper strap ¼" to wrong side (*Fig. 10*).

Fig. 10

3. Matching wrong sides and long edges, press strap in half lengthwise; open.

4. Unfold and press long raw edges to meet center crease (*Fig. 11*).

Fig. 11

5. Aligning pressed edges, refold and press again.

6. Topstitch along each edge of strap. Topstitch additional lines as desired for decorative effect.

7. Repeat Steps 1-6 to make another upper strap and two **lower straps**.

8. Repeat Steps 1 and 3-6 to make the **handle loop**. *Note: Interfacing is same length as fabric.*

MAKING THE BACKPACK BODY BACK

Note: Use a scant ¼" seam allowance to attach handle loop and straps to right side of back.

1. Fold handle loop in half. Sew each end to center top of fleece-lined backpack body back. Sew raw edges of upper straps next to handle loop (*Fig. 12*). Sew lower straps 2" from bottom of backpack body back.

Fig. 12

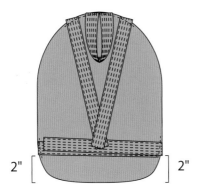

2"   2"

MAKING THE BACKPACK BODY LININGS

1. Matching right sides and short edges, fold **pocket** in half so you have a 7½" x 6" pocket; sew along short edges. Turn pocket right side out and press.

2. On right side of fabric, use the disappearing ink fabric marker to draw a line 3" from bottom edge on one backpack body lining.

3. Center pocket and align raw edges with drawn line; sew ¼" from raw edges (*Fig. 13*).

Fig. 13

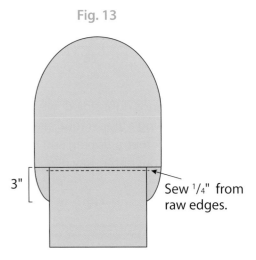

3"

Sew ¼" from raw edges.

4. Press pocket up and topstitch on each side and bottom. Sew dividing lines as desired to create pocket sections (*Fig. 14*).

Fig. 14

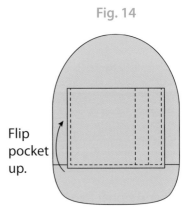

Flip pocket up.

5. Repeat Steps 1-4 for remaining backpack body lining and pocket.

MAKING THE BACKPACK

1. Fold the backpack body front in half vertically and mark the top and bottom center with a pin or disappearing ink fabric marker. Repeat with backpack body back and each backpack body lining.

2. Matching wrong sides and marked centers, pin one backpack body lining to the backpack body front. Baste together using a scant $1/4$" seam allowance *(Fig. 15)* to make front.

Fig. 15

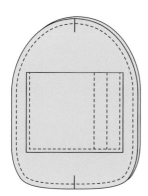

3. Repeat Steps 1-2 with backpack body back and backpack body lining to make back.

4. Make small clips (about $1/8$" deep and about 1" apart) along the raw edges of the sides *(Fig. 16)*. This will help to ease the fit around the curves.

Fig. 16

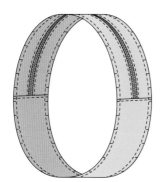

5. Matching right sides and center marks, sew the front to the sides using a $3/8$" seam allowance *(Fig. 17)* and easing to fit as needed.

Fig. 17

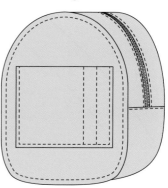

6. Repeat Step 5 to sew back to the sides, being careful not to catch straps or handle loop in stitching.

7. Matching wrong sides and long raw edges, press each **bias binding strip** in half lengthwise.

8. Press one end of each bias binding strip diagonally *(Fig. 18)*.

Fig. 18

9. Beginning with pressed end, match raw edges of one piece of binding to raw edges of one seam in backpack; pin.

10. Using a $3/8$" seam allowance, sew binding to backpack until binding overlaps beginning end by about 2". Trim excess binding.

11. Fold binding over seam allowances, covering stitching line and encasing seam allowances; pin in place.

12. Topstitch binding in place close to folded edge.

13. Repeat Steps 9-12 and use remaining binding strip to bind remaining raw edges.

14. Turn the backpack right side out through the zipper opening.

15. Slip the end of the upper strap into the female end of the buckle; fold the fabric over about $1 3/4$" and sew in place. Repeat for remaining upper strap.

16. Slip the end of the lower strap into the male end of the buckle. Repeat for remaining lower strap. The lower straps are adjustable; do not sew in place.

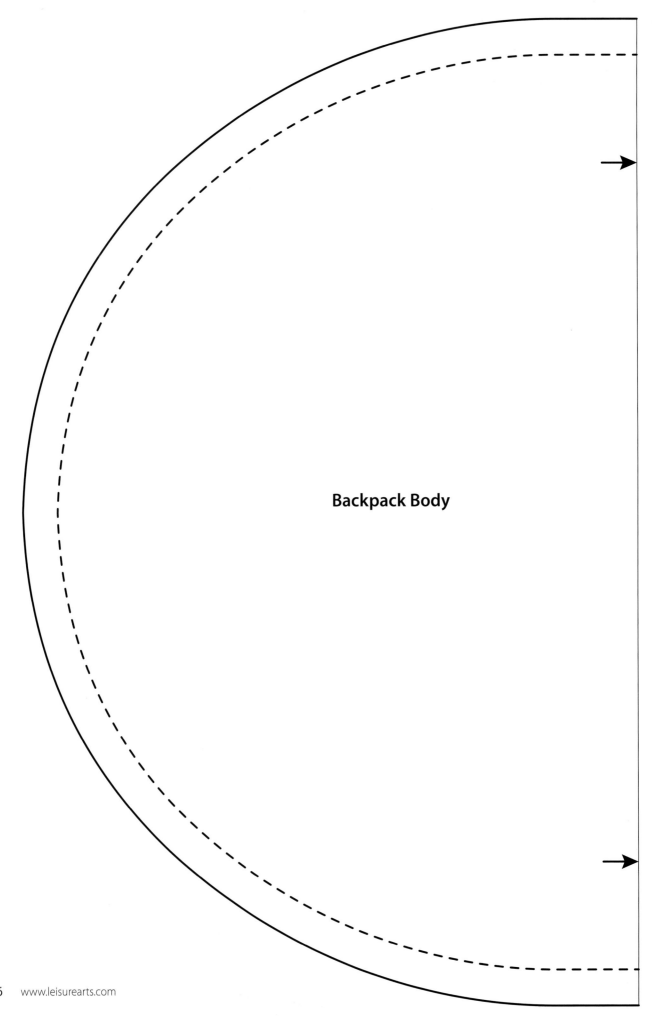

Backpack Body

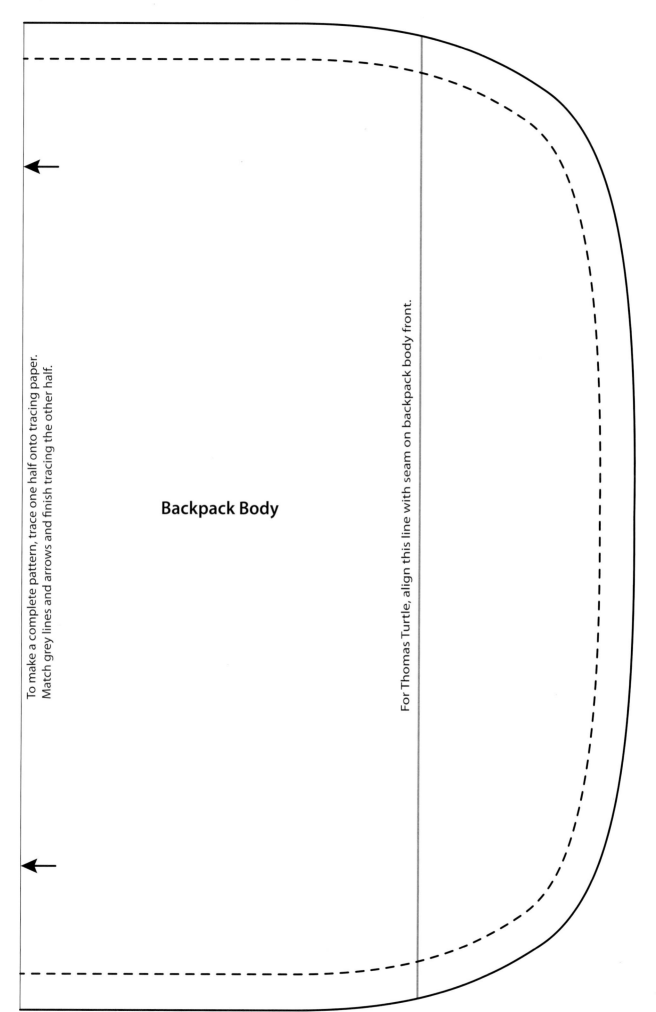

Backpack Body

To make a complete pattern, trace one half onto tracing paper.
Match grey lines and arrows and finish tracing the other half.

For Thomas Turtle, align this line with seam on backpack body front.

17

Bryson Bear

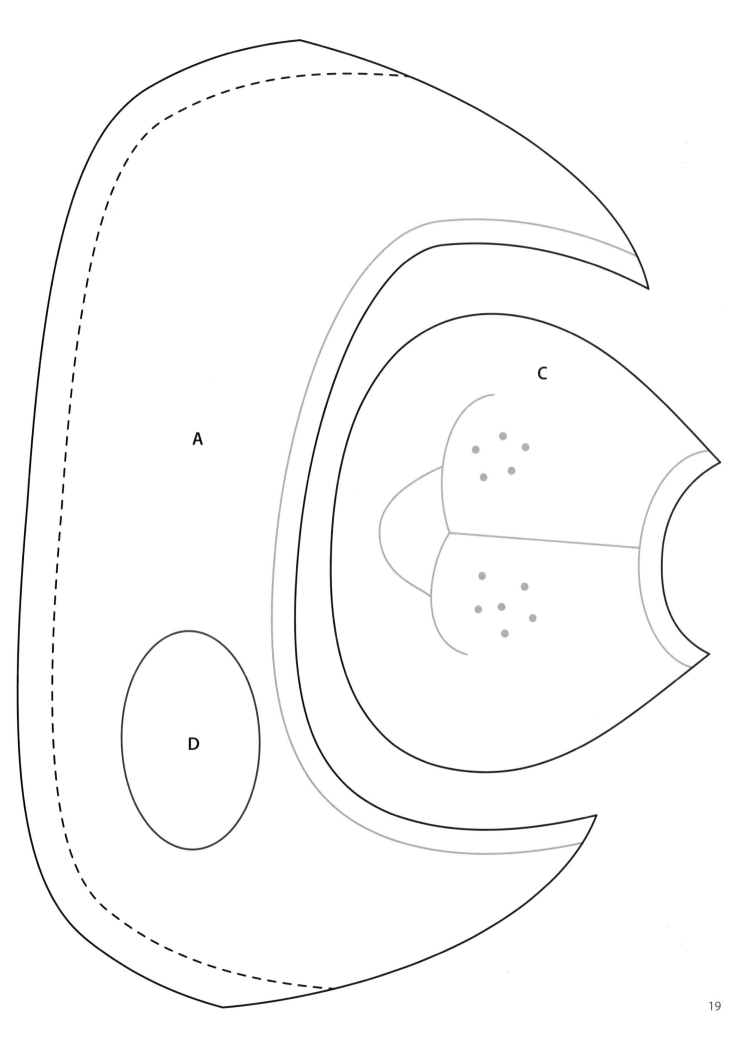

A

C

D

Filomena Fox

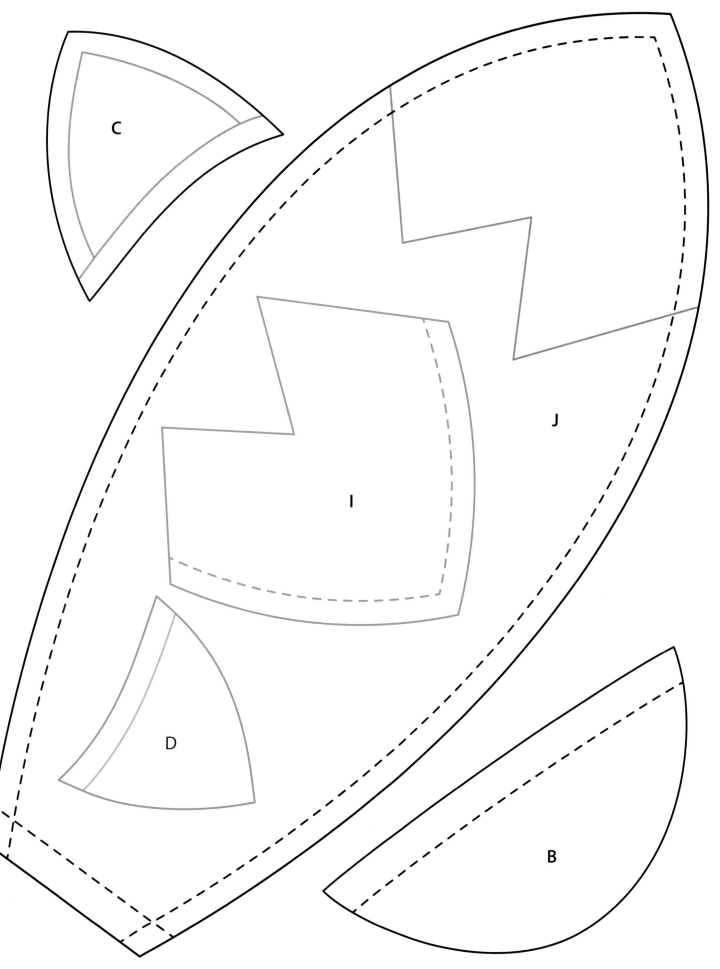

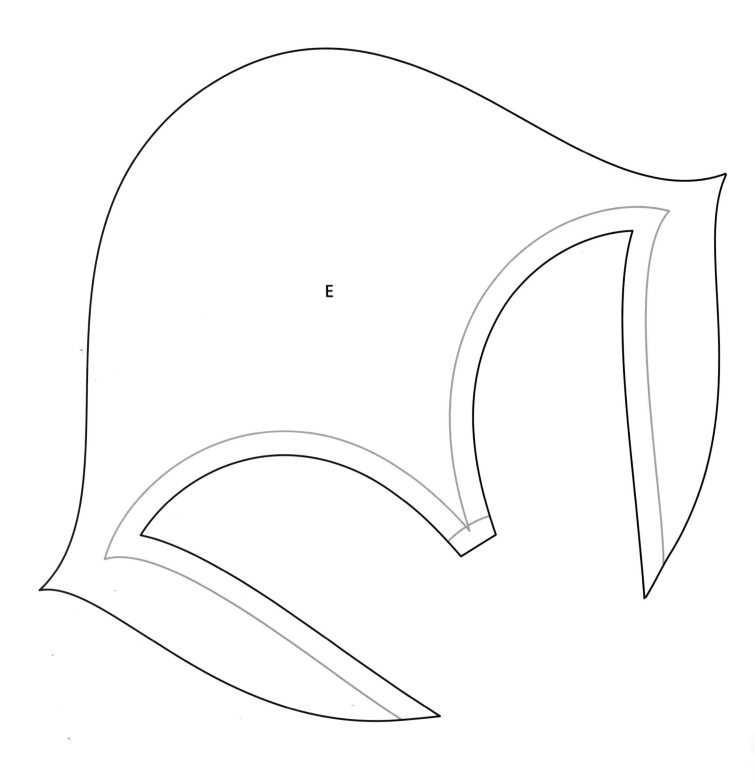

E

Thomas Turtle

P

M

L

K

J

B

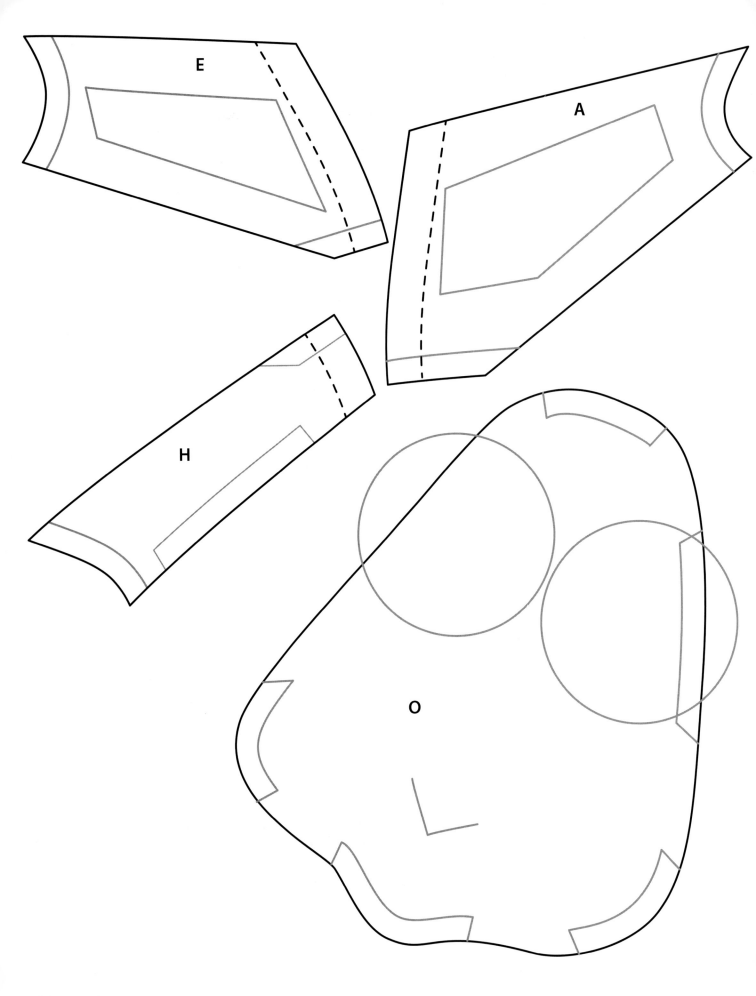

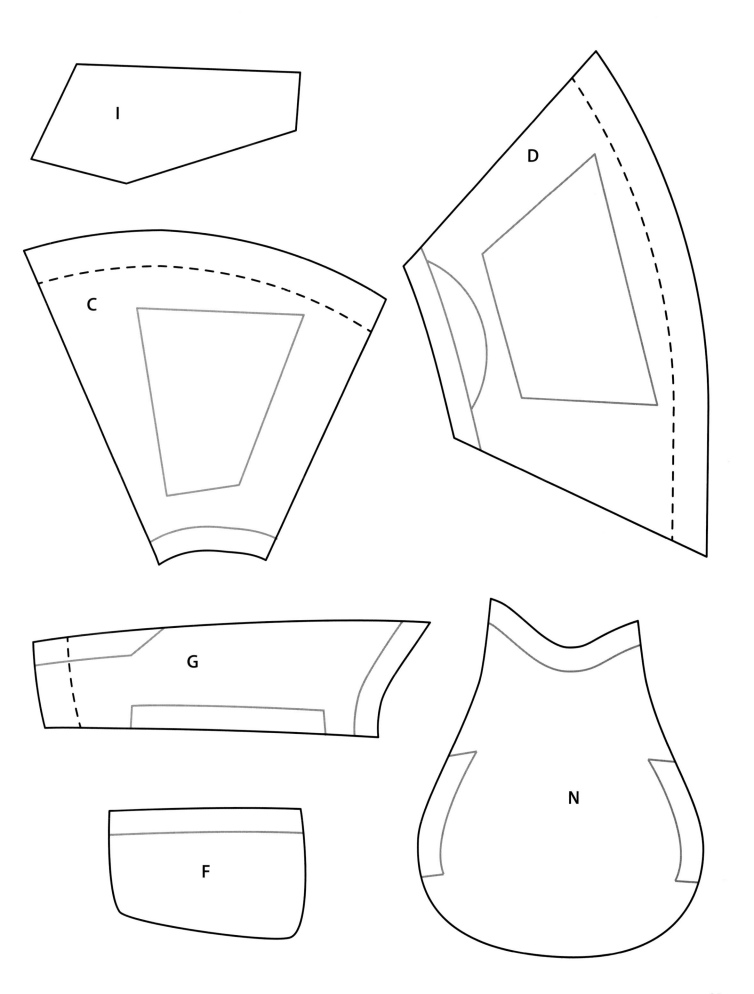

Fitzgerald Frog

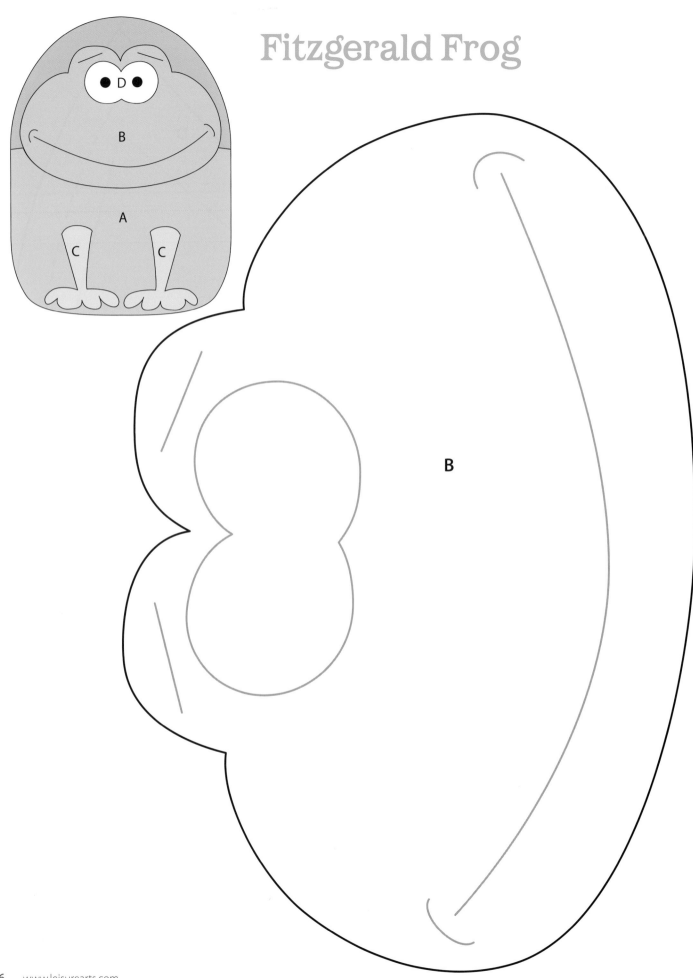

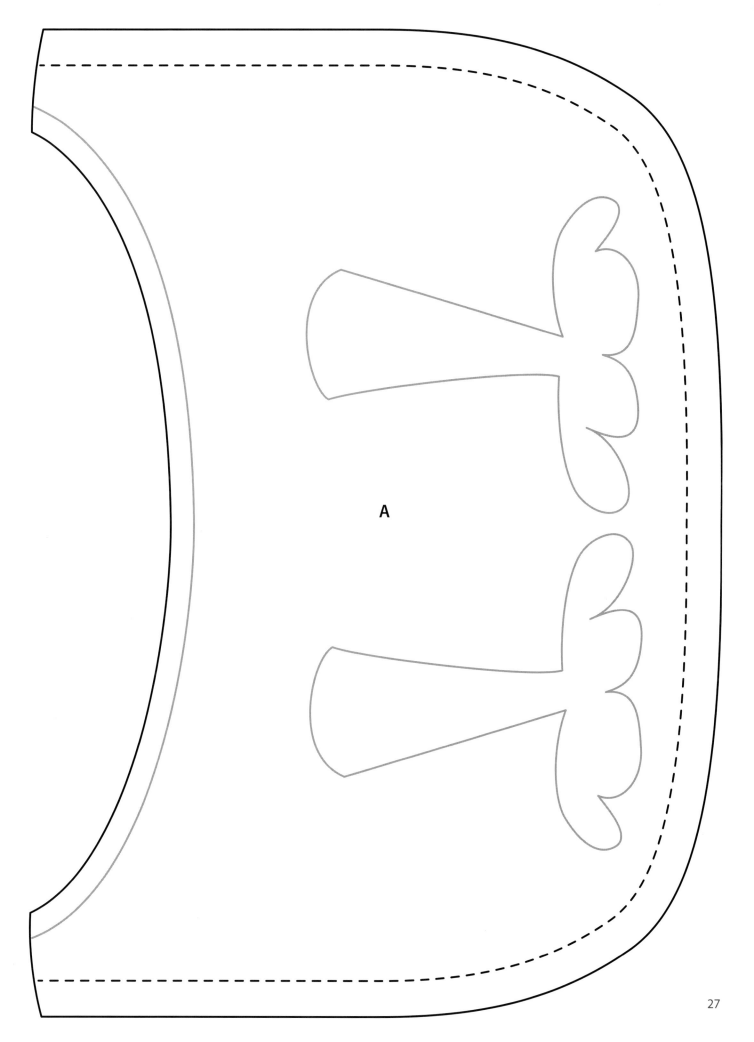

A

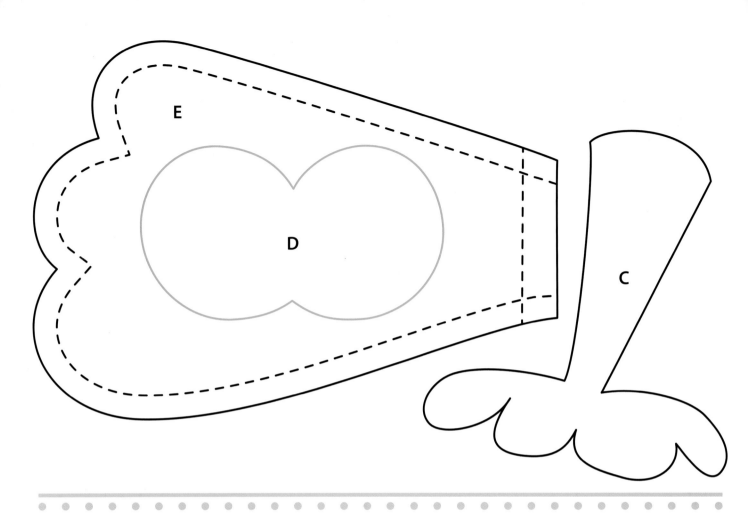

Olympia Owl

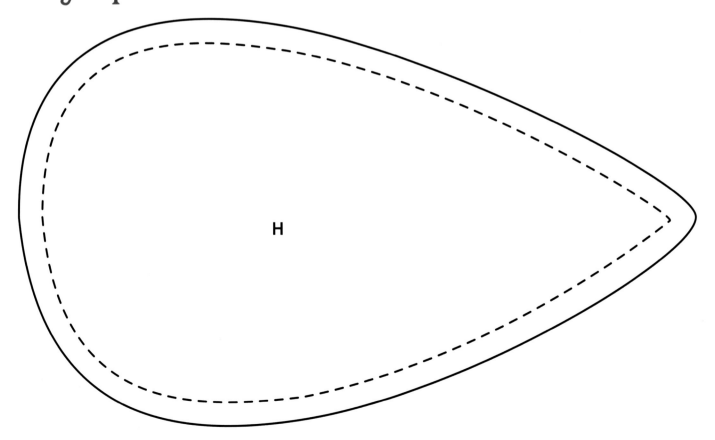

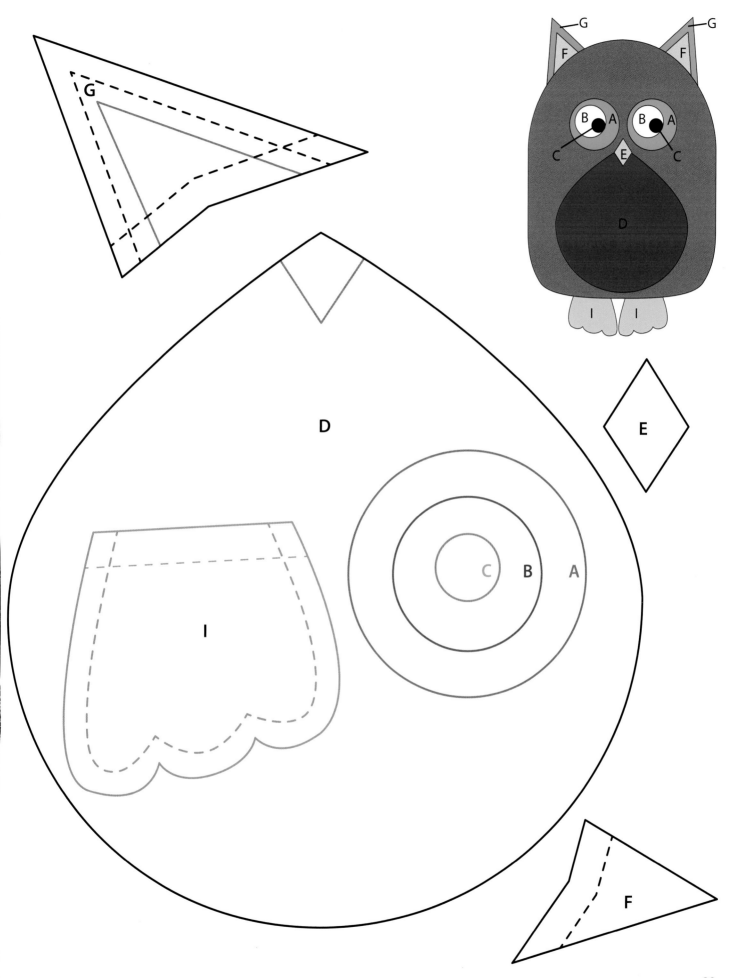

G

D

B A

C

E

F

I

29

General Instructions

To make your project easier and more enjoyable, we encourage you to carefully read **Assembling the Backpack**, pages 12-15, and the **General Instructions**, pages 30-32, study the color photographs, and familiarize yourself with the individual project instructions before beginning a project.

SELECTING FABRICS

Choose high-quality, medium-weight 100% cotton fabrics. All-cotton fabrics hold a crease better and fray less than cotton/polyester blends.

Yardage requirements listed for each project are based on 43"/44" wide fabric with a "usable" width of 40" after shrinkage and trimming selvages. Actual usable width will probably vary slightly from fabric to fabric.

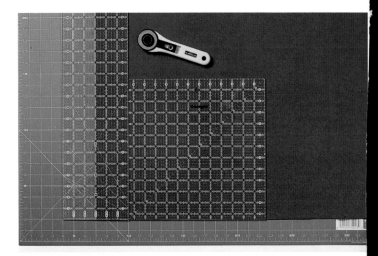
Fig. 1

PREPARING FABRICS

We recommend that all fabrics be washed, dried, and pressed before cutting. If fabrics are not pre-washed, washing the finished backpack will cause shrinkage and puckering. Bright and dark colors, which may run, should always be washed before cutting. After washing and drying fabric, fold lengthwise with wrong sides together and matching selvages.

Fig. 2

ROTARY CUTTING

• Place fabric on work surface with fold closest to you.

• Cut all strips from the selvage-to-selvage width of the fabric unless otherwise indicated in project instructions.

• Square left edge of fabric using rotary cutter and rulers *(Figs. 1-2)*.

To cut each strip required for a project, place ruler over cut edge of fabric, aligning desired marking on ruler with cut edge; make cut *(Fig. 3)*.

Fig. 3

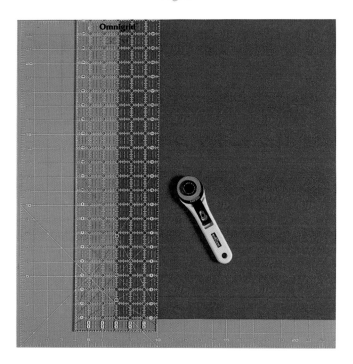

When cutting several strips from a single piece of fabric, it is important to make sure that cuts remain at a perfect right angle to the fold; square fabric as needed.

MACHINE SEWING

Set sewing machine stitch length for approximately 12 stitches per inch.

Use general-purpose sewing thread in needle and in bobbin.

An accurate seam allowance is *essential*.

When sewing, always place pieces right sides together and match raw edges and pin unless otherwise indicated.

PRESSING

- Use steam iron set on "Cotton" for all pressing.

- Press after sewing each seam.

MACHINE APPLIQUÉ

Preparing Fusible Appliqués

White or light-colored fabrics may need to be lined with fusible interfacing before applying fusible web to prevent darker fabrics from showing through. (This additional interfacing is not included in the Shopping List.)

1. Appliqué patterns are printed in reverse. Place paper-backed fusible web, paper side up, over appliqué pattern. Trace pattern onto paper side of web with pencil as many times as indicated in project instructions for a single fabric. If the appliqué is to be cut in reverse, use a black fine-point marker to trace the pattern onto plain white paper. Flip paper over and trace the pattern onto web from the "wrong" side of the paper. A light box or sunny window is helpful in doing this.
2. Follow manufacturer's instructions to fuse traced patterns to wrong side of fabrics. Do not remove paper backing.
3. Use scissors to cut out appliqué pieces along traced lines.

Satin Stitch Appliqué

A good satin stitch is a thick, smooth, almost solid line of zigzag stitching that covers the exposed raw edges of appliqué pieces.

1. Pin stabilizer, such as paper or any of the commercially available products, on wrong side of background fabric before stitching appliqués in place.
2. Thread sewing machine with general-purpose thread; use general-purpose thread that matches background fabric in bobbin.
3. Set sewing machine for a medium (approximately 1/8") zigzag stitch and a short stitch length. Slightly loosening the top tension may yield a smoother stitch.

4. Begin by stitching two or three stitches in place (drop feed dogs or set stitch length at 0) to anchor thread. Most of the Satin Stitch should be on the appliqué with the right edge of the stitch falling at the outside edge of the appliqué. Stitch over all exposed raw edges of appliqué pieces.

5. (**Note:** Dots on *Figs. 4-9* indicate where to leave needle in fabric when pivoting.) For outside corners, stitch just past corner, stopping with needle in background fabric *(Fig. 4)*. Raise presser foot. Pivot project, lower presser foot, and stitch adjacent side *(Fig. 5)*.

Fig. 4   Fig. 5

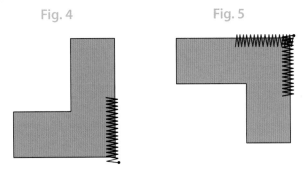

6. For inside corners, stitch just past corner, stopping with needle in appliqué fabric *(Fig. 6)*. Raise presser foot. Pivot project, lower presser foot, and stitch adjacent side *(Fig. 7)*.

Fig. 6   Fig. 7

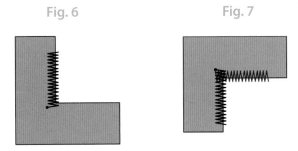

7. When stitching outside curves, stop with needle in background fabric. Raise presser foot and pivot project as needed. Lower presser foot and continue stitching, pivoting as often as necessary to follow curve *(Fig. 8)*.

Fig. 8

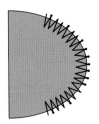

8. When stitching inside curves, stop with needle in appliqué fabric. Raise presser foot and pivot project as needed. Lower presser foot and continue stitching, pivoting as often as necessary to follow curve *(Fig. 9)*.

Fig. 9

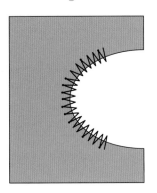

9. Do not backstitch at end of stitching. Pull threads to wrong side of background fabric; knot thread and trim ends.

10. Carefully tear away stabilizer.

Production Team: Technical Editor – Lisa Lancaster; Technical Associate – Jean Lewis; Editorial Writer - Susan Frantz Wiles; Senior Graphic Artist – Lora Puls; Graphic Artists - Cailen Cochran, Frances Huddleston, and Victoria Temple; Photostylist – Lori Wenger; Photographer - Jason Masters.

We have made every effort to ensure that these instructions are accurate and complete. We cannot, however, be responsible for human error, typographical mistakes, or variations in individual work.